Thoughts from an Introvert

Becca Webb

BookLeaf Publishing

India | USA | UK

Presentation by *BookLeaf Publishing*

Web: www.bookleafpub.com

E-mail: info@bookleafpub.com

ISBN: 9789357213981

First edition 2022

For my best friend, Morgan, who always understands the things I don't say.

For my parents, who always support me

Introvert's Dream

Self-isolation is never fun for long.
An introvert's dream is
Being alone with their thoughts,
Yet thoughts can be dangerous.

An introvert's dream is
in their own thought up world.
Yet thoughts can be dangerous
if left unchecked.

In their own thought up world,
things aren't as perfect
if left unchecked
for far too long.

Things aren't as perfect as
when all you have is yourself
for far too long
without the comfort of a friend.

When all you have is yourself—
alone with your thoughts,
without the comfort of a friend—
self-isolation is never fun.

Whispers of Silence

I surrender to the honest silence
That whispers in my direction
Telling me of the introverted sky.

"You can be found there,
Amid the wild shadows
Of the moon.

You have a place
To belong when
The darkness invades.

The stars will shine
For you to see
What is hidden from your eyes.

You will find what you seek
When you lift your eyes to the introverted
Sky that cannot fade."

My fear breaks,
As I hope
The silence won't lie to me.

Silence and Secrets

Silence, never ending
All consuming
A gift, a fear
I hate to sit in silence
Music is my friend
But sometimes I need
To sit in the silence
To hear the whispers
I can't miss

Secrets buried deep
Never to be said
Out loud
Dark and true
We want to keep
Them inside
But they want
To be screamed
From the rooftop
Who wins?

Are silence and secrets
Friends or enemies?
Do they work together
Or against each other?

Are they essential or burdens?
Are they even real?

Desperate for Peace

If you saw me daydreaming as I strolled through
the ferns
you would know I was wishing to return to the
peace of Hemlock Haven.

If I forgot too quickly
you would surround me with my memories.

If I wandered too far you would bring me back.
If I thought too much
you would ground me again. If my mind lost its
sight

you would paint me a picture, you would sing
the song of summer, you would share all your
secrets.

If you saw me picking the wildflowers of the
meadow
you would know how much I feel like I
belonged.

If I left without turning to look at the wishing
tree,

if I drove away on my own without saying
goodbye

you'll know I always will return in my dreams
to the place I once knew so well that I can't
reach now.

Seeking Memories

Depend, you say, I can depend on you.
Suspense is all you give to me. Forget
The idea I will return. Who knew
the time would come I would choose to regret.

Defense, I need to defend myself from
every single thought I can't keep hidden.
My mind's weakness, as I run away numb,
Calls me back. I wish this was unwritten

That longing to go flying through the ghost
of us. As I circle continuously
I am reminded of how close almost
was to us. Yet we individually

chose the paths we took through the fog, keeping
us to only memories left seeking.

Remember or Forget

8

Why can't I remember:
The reason I started there,
The feeling I had when I met you -
My first impression of you?

I know how much
You meant to me,
How much happiness I found there
When I remember the good.

I wish I knew then
What I know now,
But if I did
Would I still have worked there?

If I saw you for
Who you would become
Would I still try
To save our friendship?

Why can't I forget:
The reason I left there,
The jokes we had,
My favorite memories?

I know how much
You hurt me,
How much pain I felt then
When I reflect on it now.

If I knew I would
Never forget the hurt
Would I still choose
You and that place?

If I could return to then
To that first year
Would I leave
When you did?

Could that solve everything?

Dear Lost Love

I'm not writing to the love you feel
Like butterflies in your stomach
When you look across the table
At the one you want to see everyday

I'm writing to the love that comes
Only for season
As friends come and go
The love that stays
Though people left
Long ago

That love the one you can't forget
Do you even want to?
The love stays in the memories of the people
The ones untainted by the ending

To that love I want to say
I still feel it deep in my soul
Though I haven't seen them in years
I don't you back in my life
I don't want to go back
I may wonder what if
But I know its better
This way

So to love I wish
You all best I hope
You're moving forward
To better things and places
Than when I knew you
I may never know if you ever
Think of me but I want to know
I understand now how we came to this

The love that lasts beyond the season
When the friendships leaves
With the wind of change
I'm holding on to that love
While letting go
Of the people who
Inspired it

Listen

I've always thought I was a good listener.
I'm naturally quiet, so it's easy – most of the
time
But sometimes
I don't want to.
She comes mind.

I never wanted to listen.
Why should I?
She never did.
In hindsight she deserved a chance,
to make things right,
to know why.

I think back to the day I started to see
Something was wrong.
She told me her secret and I kept mine.
I kept a lot from her,
Including the day, I said,
"Goodbye."

Love

A feeling lost to some, yet
Others know it too well.
He'll wait to go until
She is taken care of.
She cooks for him before work.
A friend's embrace, the gift of
Thoughtful words, knowing you're
In their memories, the happy ones.

Family Gift

I have a saying that I use quite frequently.
A gift my parents gave me inspired it:
"Genetics cursed me." There is only one
thing every parent gives their child.
Genes, DNA; it was that gift which cursed me.
Weak ankles, random knee pain, the inevitable
hip issues
all a gift from my parents to me.
It's funny now. I've fallen down the stairs
more times than I can count.
I have to watch everywhere I walk
or I'll trip on nothing at all.
A twisted ankle is no problem. It happens
monthly.
I can deal with ankle and knee pain more than I
should.
I don't think twice if twist an ankle, just put on
brace.
My genes may have cursed me, but they
were a gift nonetheless, so thanks.

Grandfathers Gone

I don't remember much about the life
five-year-old me lived,
But I do remember it including my first
experience with death.
I had never seen my father cry before the day his
father died.
Health issues plagued my grandfather.
I can't tell you which illness killed him, but
I can say Pappy lived a good life full of love and
happiness.
It's a shame I don't remember much about him.

I remember sixteen-year-old me, as we all
watched
Cancer take over my mom's father.
With each day his face lost some brightness.
Pop lasted almost two years.
We never expected that much time was left for
him.
Knowing death could come at any time, and
powerlessly waiting for it,
It's almost worse than my first grandfather's
sudden death. Maybe,
I felt it more now that I understood death as it is.
The day Pop passed,

Was so different than when Pappy died. I was
waiting for cancer to win.
We knew it was going to be soon. We didn't
know how he was still fighting.
The doctors said he shouldn't have still been
with us.
That night I was mad for being at work, but for
the wrong reason.
I wanted to be at homecoming game, but I
should have been home.
I didn't know until seven hours after when I left
work.
The tears came fast, but I never really processed
it
until the weekend had passed and I could stop
to remember him and feel the weight of his
passing.

Now both my grandfathers are gone, and I know
death is hard
To process; and it's hard to move without them,
but we must.

Susquehanna Father

The Susquehanna River has stories to tell.
I grew up on that river just as he did.
It twists and turns and never stays still.
The Susquehanna always has something else to
do,
Somewhere it wants to be.
It changes as fast as a storm roles in.

The river has its scars:
The rocks that only sometimes come
Up to the surface,
The secrets hidden under the water
Only seen on the rare
Clear days.

Still the river is home.
It is honest in its goal,
Its expectations.
It will travel far and do anything
For the life it holds inside.
I always find peace beside the waters
That forever flow on
Towards a place unknown in the moment
That will be its home.

River

I was raised on this river, like you were.
I remember pieces about the island,
The stories live, though sometimes a blur.
Smiles come easy on water.

Dryland is where it gets harder, more problems
arise.
The only problem on water is the rocks
Lurking beneath the surface,
a surprise waiting to hinder our trip to the dock.

Now I sit on the dock, patient, searching,
For what I'm not sure,
      Answers,
      Minnows
Depends how deep I want to go.
I'm sure of this, here is my window,

Through which I see the past, the life you lived
Through which I know I can be relieved.

Hemlock Haven

I miss it every day
I've never been able to get it out of my mind
Hemlock Haven, my favorite place

Maybe it's because it reminds me of him
Or maybe it's the mountain air
The beauty of undisturbed nature
The chances of seeing a deer or bear

Maybe it's the streams and the pond
I spent most of my time walking in the water
Hiding in the forest around it
Fishing in the pond and
Trying to catch salamanders

I was still a kid when we left it behind
But I still picture every room
Every part of the property
I can still imagine
I was there
I was at home in
Hemlock Haven.

Spring

i watch and wait,
longing for your arrival
for the world to be brighter.

you are patient
knowing you'll be appreciated more.
it will come with
lilacs.
raindrops.
butterflies.

you are on your way and
i am learning to be patient.

SPRING

Puzzle

**Inspired by Louis Comfort Tiffany's Mosaic
"Garden Landscape"**

Serenity in perfect picture,
Floating on the ever-flowing lake.
Peace in eternal calmness,
Adding a splash of color to glassy water.

Thousands of pieces fitted together
In the mosaic of a garden.
Each with its ideal placement,
Adding to the truthful image.

I wish I had seen
this scene so inspired,
But now it sits on a wall,
Viewed by thousands every day.

The swans live on
Surrounded by rainbow reflections,
With heaven calling home
The lost that have been found.

The water stills,
Yet flows on,

As we wait like the lake,
As we live like the fountain.

Where do I fit in the puzzle?

See the Light

For years I've watched the night slowly turn to
day
Wishing it would all go away
I've seen the darkness close in
All around it's hard to find the light
Where it all begins

Well they say a journey begins with one single
step
They say in the end it'll all be ok
Well I know now that someday I'll turn back
And say the pain I felt that day
I can't feel it anymore
It's an open door

Sometimes I think of the before
Wishing I could have changed those days
And all those years ago
Is a time I've found to be
My golden dream

And yet they still say a journey begins with one
single step
They say in the end it'll all be ok
And I know someday I'll turn back

And say the pain I felt that day
I can't feel it anymore
Life is an open door

For we are living life on the Earth
We are all fighting battles
fought before
We have all found a tunnel
where the darkness it closes in
The struggle to find the light
 is here again

And yet they still say that a journey begins with
one single step
They say in the end it'll all be ok
And I know that someday I'll turn back
And say the pain I felt that day
I can't feel it anymore

And one thing's for sure
We have all wished upon a star
A wish we never told
We have all dreamed of freedom from the
darkness
We have all hoped and
We have all longed for the light's return
It'll be here soon I'm sure

For they say that a journey begins with a single
step
And in the end it'll all be ok
I know someday I can turn back
And say that the pain I felt that day
I can't feel it anymore

And I see light before me
The darkness it has left
I've stepped out into the open again
And the tunnel behind me
Falls to the ground
And all around the darkness
Is nowhere to be found

Stand Firm

Why? When?
Millions of questions spin
Round and round my head
Where? Who?
I don't have my answers yet
I haven't lost hope though
I know you've heard my prayers
I know I'll get my answers someday

I won't give up
I'll stand firm
Just like you've asked
Even though
I don't know why
Why all this
I don't know when
When it'll all be done
I don't know where
Where I'm meant to be
I don't know who
Who I'm supposed to be
But I know You
And You know me

I know You have your plans

And I'll trust it
I know you're telling me to wait,
To trust, to believe in You
I know it'll all work out
I know it's all worth it
But I still have questions
I can't stop them now
I've heard you whispers
Through the silence

So I'll stand firm
Just like you asked
Even though
I don't know why
Why all this
I don't know when
When it'll all be done
I don't know where
Where I'm meant to be
I don't know who
Who I'm supposed to be
But I know You
And You know me

Everyone says I'll be fine,
That I don't have to worry
And I know they're right
I don't want to be this way
It's just hard sometimes

To push it all away
I tell myself
Keep trying
Don't give in
Maybe sometimes it's better
To pretend

But I'll stand firm
Just like you asked
Even though
I don't know why
Why all this
I don't know when
When it'll all be done
I don't know where
Where I'm meant to be
I don't know who
Who I'm supposed to be
But I know You
And You know me

You know me
If nothing else
I know You
And You know me
You know me

Ghost

Some say they don't exist,
But I know they do.
I've felt their presence for years.
No, not the ghosts of stories or research,
What I mean is the ghosts
Of the past.

Places, people, objects
They all leave their mark,
Marks that can be felt for centuries.
I have my ghosts.
Do you?

Past places are strong.
I remember some well.
Potter County is a place.
God's country they call it.
I never knew why,
But it sure felt like heaven sometimes.
Hemlock Haven,
My favorite place
It was my family's.
So many memories,
Memories of games
We were so competitive.

Of forest walks
So beautiful
Everywhere took
My breath away.
Of four wheeler rides
And learning to drive
In an open field
Nothing to hit
Just an ATV to ride
Through the mountains
Sometimes flat meadows
Sometimes bumpy hills.
I remember the creek
And the pond
Oh how cold that pond was
Even in July.
That place lives on in mind
And in memories,
But now it's a ghost to me.
November 4, 2013
It's death date.

People come and go.
In life they leave.
In memory they stay.
She was my everything.
My best friend now
And forever.
Some days she feel like a ghost though.

I hardly see her.
Four hours away
She lives,
But here she is a ghost,
That never ceases to haunt me.
My thoughts go to her.
She is alive and a ghost
At the same time.
Seven years this way

Objects lost
Can seem unimportant,
But I know of some
I'll never forget.
A necklace in particular
Comes to mind
It came in a DVD case,
Princess Protection Program
A silver crown split in half
BFF written there
I still remember after eight years.
What this meant
The pain it brought
The story it uncovered
All of it carved into my brain.
Never to be forgotten.
Even though the object
Remains lost, maybe broken.
I'll never find it,

But I'll never forget it either.
Thanks to its ghost.

Places, people, objects
They all leave their mark,
Marks that can be felt for centuries
As ghosts of the past.
Now that you know my story.
Do you believe in ghosts?

Sky Blue

Sky Blue
Sky's the Limit
I miss you more
With Each day.
You taught me more
Then even I know.
With you I flew
Through the sky,
Like I could
Touch the clouds.
I'll never forget
The blue ribbon
You chose as the best.
I tried to be okay
When you were gone.
I never made it
To the saddle.
Instead, I cried the whole
Way home.
Sky you're in the
Stable in the sky.
May you jump
To your heart's content.
Forever in my mind,
Forever in my heart,

As the horse
I loved
Most.

Before I Go

The time is coming
What's light at the end
Of the tunnel to me
May seem to be darkness
Approaching to you
So before I go
There's some things
You must know

I'm doing this me
For my dreams
But home will always be
That same house
I've always know
On that hill
I hated to climb
With the people
Who I will forever love

Distance doesn't break
What it separates
You've witnessed that
Already in my life

I was born with a spirit

To travel
For adventure
This my next one
Someday I'll come home
Maybe not how you wish
Maybe not when you wish
But know I will come home
And I will always
Love you